Eco Alert!
WATER SUPPLY

Rebecca Hunter

FRANKLIN WATTS
LONDON•SYDNEY

First published in 2010 by
Franklin Watts
338 Euston Road
London NW1 3BH

Franklin Watts Australia
Level 17/207 Kent Street
Sydney NSW 2000

© 2010 Franklin Watts

ISBN 978 0 7496 9322 0

Dewey classification number: 363.6'1

A CIP catalogue record for this publication
is available from the British Library.

Planning and production by
Discovery Books Limited
Managing Editor: Rachel Tisdale
Editor: Rebecca Hunter
Designer: Blink Media
Picture research: Tom Humphrey
Illustrations: Stefan Chabluk

Printed in China

Franklin Watts is a division
of Hachette Children's Books,
an Hachette UK Company.
www.hachette.co.uk

Photographs: **Corbis:** page 5 top (Gideon Mendel),
page 5 bottom (Daniel Mirer), page 7 (Frans
Lanting), page 15 (Carol Cohen), page 24
(Atlantide Phototravel), page 27 (Bodo Marks/dpa);
Getty Images: cover (Dan Kitwood), page 11
(Dario Mitidiere), page 12 (China Photos), page 13
(Peter Martell/AFP), page 18 (Jonathan Wood),
page 20 (STR/AFP), page 22 (Guang Niu), page 29
(Thomas Kitchin & Victoria Hurst); **NASA:** page 8
top; **Rebecca Hunter:** page 28; **Shutterstock:**
page 4 (Tish1), page 9 (Shkanov Alexey), page 17
(Johanna Goodyear), page 19 (Steve Estvanik),
page 23 (Bryan Busovicki); **Wikimedia:** page 14
(Ildar Sagdejev), page 25 (Fakharany).

Contents

Water on tap

Most of us take water for granted. We turn on the tap when we want a drink. We have a bath or shower every day, and we turn on machines to wash our clothes or dishes. We simply expect water to be there whenever we want it.

Imagine what would happen if you turned on the tap and nothing happened! Suppose your water supply just ran out? You would have to collect rainwater to wash with, and join queues of people waiting for fresh water to drink.

As the population of the world increases, the worldwide demand for water is growing. It is not just drinking water that the world needs, it is water for agriculture and manufacturing industries. Did you know that it takes 140 litres of water to produce one cup of coffee? Or 3,000 litres to make a hamburger, and 8,000 litres to create a pair of leather shoes? All of these processes require enormous amounts of water to grow crops, feed cows or produce leather.

⊙ Many farms in developed countries use large quantities of water to **irrigate** their crops. Much of this is wasted in **run-off** and **evaporation**.

4

In dry places, such as parts of Africa, many homes do not have running water. These people in Zambia, have to travel long distances every day to fetch water for their families.

Unfortunately water is not distributed evenly across the world. In many countries where water is plentiful, people often waste it. In other countries many people do not have enough water. Water is a valuable global **resource** and everyone should help look after it by using it carefully and wasting less.

Families in New Jersey, USA enjoy a day out at a water theme park. People in developed parts of the world rarely suffer water shortages and may take water for granted.

The water cycle

The water on the Earth is always on the move – it is constantly being recycled. Water moves between rivers and land, the oceans and the **atmosphere**. This continuous movement of water is called the water cycle.

No beginning or end

The water cycle is a true cycle, which means there is no beginning or end. The cycle is driven by the Sun, which heats the water in the oceans and the surface water on the land. The water evaporates and becomes **water vapour**. As the water vapour rises it becomes cooler and **condenses** to form clouds.

Air currents move the clouds around the world and eventually the water falls back to the surface as rain, snow, sleet or hail. Water that falls on land either soaks in and becomes **groundwater**, or finds its way back into rivers and lakes. Some of it falls as snow on mountains or at the poles. It may stay frozen here for thousands of years before melting and rejoining the cycle.

ⓥ This diagram shows how the water cycle works.

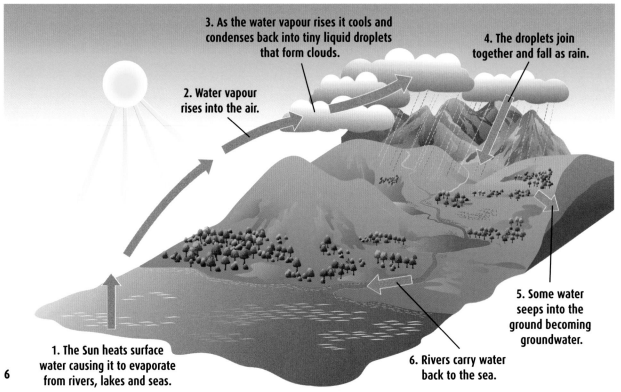

3. As the water vapour rises it cools and condenses back into tiny liquid droplets that form clouds.

2. Water vapour rises into the air.

4. The droplets join together and fall as rain.

1. The Sun heats surface water causing it to evaporate from rivers, lakes and seas.

5. Some water seeps into the ground becoming groundwater.

6. Rivers carry water back to the sea.

The water cycle can clearly be seen in action in a **rainforest** where it rains every day. Trees absorb water through their roots and give off moisture from their leaves. Clouds gather above the tree tops eventually bringing more rain, some of which reaches the rivers.

Ancient water

The fact that Earth's water is always recycled means that there is never any new water added to the cycle, nor is any ever lost. The water in the glass of squash you drank today may have fallen as rain on the other side of the world last year or could have been part of the Atlantic Ocean when Columbus sailed to America in 1492!

Taking water out

Human actions alter the water cycle by temporarily removing water from it. Water is taken out for farming, industry, power stations, **hydroelectric** power (HEP) and for domestic use. Although the water finds its way back into the water cycle eventually, the amount taken out increases every year. It is also not replaced instantly. When water is pumped from groundwater, it can take thousands of years for water to replenish these reserves.

How can you help?

Use a watering can to water your garden rather than a hose or sprinkler. Lawn sprinklers use as much water in half an hour as an average family of four does in a day.

The blue planet

When astronauts first looked down at planet Earth from space, they were astonished at how blue it looked. This was because most of what they could see was water. Now Earth is sometimes referred to as the 'blue planet'.

Water everywhere

The oceans cover a large part of the Earth's surface – about 71 per cent. They are also very deep; the Pacific Ocean has an average depth of 4.2km and the Atlantic Ocean is about 3.7km deep. Mount Everest, the highest mountain on Earth, is more than 1.5km shorter than the deepest part of the Pacific.

Since there is so much water on Earth, it seems strange to think that we could run short of it. The reason for this is that nearly all the water on Earth is salty – only 3 per cent is fresh water.

⬤ When you look at a photograph of Earth from space, you wonder why we don't rename the planet 'Water'!

◀ Most of the Earth's water is seawater. Only a small percentage is fresh water, and most of this is in ice and the ground.

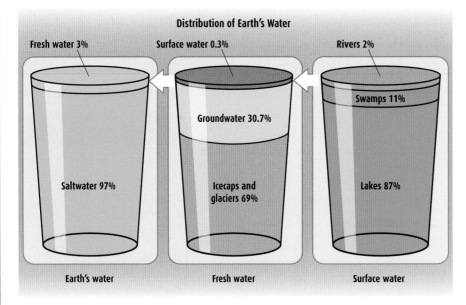

Distribution of Earth's Water

Fresh water 3% Surface water 0.3% Rivers 2%

Groundwater 30.7%

Swamps 11%

Saltwater 97%

Icecaps and glaciers 69%

Lakes 87%

Earth's water Fresh water Surface water

Fresh water

Of our fresh water, most – about 69 per cent – is locked up in ice caps and glaciers, mainly in Greenland and Antarctica. Another 30 per cent is beneath our feet in the ground. Of all the fresh water on Earth, only about 0.3 per cent is in lakes, rivers and the soil. This is the amount that is readily available for us to use and it is regularly renewed by rain and snowfall.

⊙ The Great Lakes of North America contain an estimated 23,000 cubic km of water – a fifth of all the surface fresh water on Earth.

Distribution of water

One of the problems with our water supply is the uneven distribution of it across the world. Some countries have high rainfall and large stores of water in the form of rivers and lakes. Others have little, or irregular rainfall and in hot climates water supplies dry up quickly.

Supply and demand

As well as the uneven distribution of water, the world also has an uneven distribution of people. Often large populations of people live in the areas of least water. But the reverse also occurs. Asia has the largest proportion of the world's fresh water supply, while Australia has the lowest. But Asia has a huge population and so suffers water shortages while Australia actually has the highest supply of fresh water per person because it has a very low population.

This table shows the distribution of the world's population and the available fresh water across six continents.		
Continent	Proportion of world's human population/%	Proportion of world's available fresh water/%
North and Central America	8	15
South America	6	25
Europe	12	8
Africa	13	11
Asia	60	36
Australia and Oceania	1	5

Water scarcity

The International Water Management Institute estimates that one third of the world's population face some form of **water scarcity**. They have divided water scarcity into two types: physical scarcity and economic scarcity. Physical scarcity occurs when there is not enough water in an area to meet the needs of its population. This happens in **arid** areas but can also occur in areas of plentiful water when it is badly used or wasted. Economic scarcity happens in areas with plenty of water but where the countries are too poor to put in the required **infrastructure** needed to collect, store and distribute water.

◀ Many people around the world suffer some form of water scarcity. Here Kampuchean refugees queue for water at a camp in Thailand, Asia.

◉ This map shows which areas of the world suffer from some form of water scarcity.

Little or no water scarcity

Approaching physical water scarcity

Physical water scarcity

Economic water scarcity

No data available

Drinking water

Most plants and animals are composed mainly of water and no living thing can survive without it.

A basic human right

Since water is essential to life, it should be a basic human right. However, despite many international agreements over human rights, the right to fresh water has largely been ignored, perhaps because the scale of the problem is so enormous. Not everyone has access to water, and for millions the quantity and quality is insufficient to survive.

How much do we need?

Human beings need a minimum of 3–5 litres of clean water a day to survive. However, studies have shown that basic health is improved if people have 20 litres per person per day. This allows for basic **sanitation** as well as the water in food and drink. If you allow for bathing and for preparing and cooking food, then a figure of 50 litres per person per day is a more realistic minimum.

⊙ Over one billion people in the world do not have clean, safe running water in their homes. Many, like these women in China, have to wash their clothes in the river. They may have to get their drinking water from here as well.

Who has enough?

In **developed countries**, people use far more than the minimum 50 litres suggested. In the UK an average of 200 litres per day is consumed, while in the USA people use an average of 500 litres per day. People in 62 **developing countries**, including India, Kenya and Jamaica live on less than 50 litres a day, with the lowest, Haiti and The Gambia, having just 3 litres per day – barely enough to survive.

Water and health

The supply of clean water is affected by how people dispose of their dirty water, including **sewage**. People living in areas where there is no sanitation system for the disposal of waste water have little choice but to throw it away or into a river. This leads to the spread of diseases such as **cholera** and **typhoid** and diarrhoea.

⊙ More than half of the hospital beds in the world are occupied by people suffering from water-borne diseases. These patients are recovering at the Akobo hospital in Sudan, Africa.

HOTSPOT:

World Water Day

In 1992, the United Nations General Assembly designated 22 March as World Water Day. Every year on this date, people throughout the world participate in events to promote the conservation and development of global water resources.

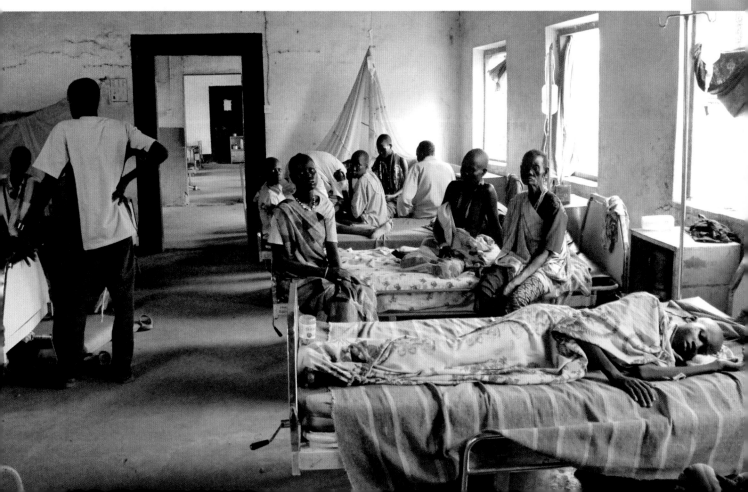

Agriculture

Most of the demand for water in the world comes from agriculture, which accounts for 70 per cent of global water use. Water is used in agriculture in two main ways to irrigate crops and to rear livestock.

Irrigation

Irrigation is the supply of water to land in order to grow crops. It allows more crops to be grown on an area, and for crops to be grown in places that would otherwise be too dry. Many methods of crop irrigation are very wasteful of water. On some irrigated farms less than half the water actually reaches the plants, the rest is lost in leaks, evaporation or is soaked up by surrounding soil. Farmers can improve their irrigation **efficiency** by repairing leaks and using low-energy sprinklers or drip irrigation. This reduces water loss to less than 10 per cent.

HOTSPOT:

Wasteful lawns!

Lawns are one of the world's biggest wasters of water. In the USA they cover over 160,000 square km of land, and consume 1,000 billion litres of water a week, making them the country's largest agricultural sector!

Rearing livestock

Rearing livestock demands even more water than growing crops. The grass and feed that the animals eat have to be grown and the animals also require large amounts of drinking water. One bullock drinks on average 63 litres of water a day. It takes over 15,000 litres of water to produce one kilogram of beef!

⊕ Drip irrigation is the most water-efficient method of irrigation but it is also the most expensive. In this vineyard in California, USA, water is dripped onto the base of the plants at regular intervals so very little is lost in evaporation or run-off.

Different types of food production need different quantities of water. This table shows how much water is needed to produce 1 kilogram of different foodstuffs.	
	Litres of water
Potatoes	500 to 1,500
Wheat	900 to 2,000
Rice	1,900 to 5,000
Chicken	3,500 to 5,700
Beef	15,000 to 70,000

How can you help?

Become a vegetarian! A meat-eater uses three times more water in their meals than a vegetarian does. Even if you don't want to give up meat completely, reducing the amount you eat will help conserve water.

Industry

After agriculture, industry is the next biggest global user of water. Over 22 per cent of fresh water is used in industry and this figure is set to double by 2025. In rapidly industrialising countries like China, it could increase by up to five times.

Water at work

Ever since the **Industrial Revolution**, water has been one of the most important resources in industry. Factories use water in many ways, such as to wash, cool and drive machinery. Large industries that are very dependant on water are often located close to rivers or other water sources.

This chart shows how different countries use their water supply in different ways.

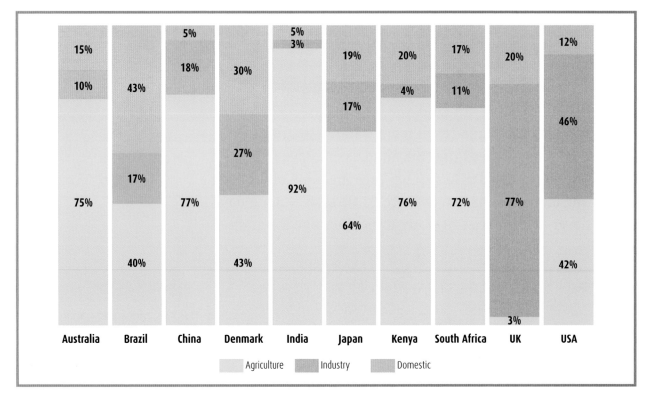

	Australia	Brazil	China	Denmark	India	Japan	Kenya	South Africa	UK	USA
Domestic	15%	43%	5%	30%	5%	19%	20%	17%	20%	12%
Industry	10%	17%	18%	27%	3%	17%	4%	11%	77%	46%
Agriculture	75%	40%	77%	43%	92%	64%	76%	72%	3%	42%

Legend: Agriculture · Industry · Domestic

Biggest water users

Three of the largest industrial users of water are the **textile**, steel and paper-making industries. Each of these requires huge quantities of water to make its products.

Manufacturing one tonne of steel requires 20,000 litres of water, while a tonne of paper can use a staggering 90,000 litres.

Although industry uses a massive amount of water, it employs many more people and it produces a greater quantity of end products than agriculture. For example, in California, USA, the amount of water needed to support 100,000 technical jobs would support fewer than ten jobs in farming.

⊕ A pulp and paper mill on the edge of the Humber River in Newfoundland, Canada. The paper-making industry uses enormous amounts of water so traditionally factories have always been situated on the banks of rivers.

Saving water

Many industries have started making dramatic cuts in the amount of water they consume. As well as improving their manufacturing processes, simple procedures such as replacing worn pipes, fixing leaks and monitoring tanks to ensure they don't overflow, have all lowered water consumption. Saving water also means these industries are saving money.

HOTSPOT:

Swedish paper industry

Since 1990 the Swedish paper industry has not only doubled the amount of paper it makes, but also halved the amount of water it uses!

Climate change

Many people worry that human actions are causing **global warming** which will in turn bring a change in climate. Rainfall patterns could change all over the world bringing more rain to some areas but less to others.

Droughts in Africa

Africa is the second driest continent in the world, and at present millions of Africans suffer from water shortages throughout the year. If climate change predictions are correct, nearly 50 per cent of Africa's population will face water scarcity by the year 2025. Farmers will not have enough water for their crops and **yields** could drop by a half. This will make Africa even more dependent on international aid.

▽ Australia is the driest continent and is currently suffering from the worst drought on record. This is thought to be a result of changing weather patterns caused by global warming. Thousands of farmers face ruin as irrigation is stopped and crops and livestock die.

Water from snow and ice

Climate change will cause major water shortages for millions of people in Asia and South America who rely on water supplies from melting snow and glaciers. Rising temperatures mean that there will be more rain and less snow in the mountains, and also that the snow will melt earlier in the year causing water shortages later on. The Himalayan glaciers are already melting faster. This will lead to huge problems for the hundreds of millions of people in China, Nepal and India who rely on the water for drinking and for irrigating their crops.

Increased flooding

Too much water can be as big a problem as too little. Flooding can be caused by rising sea levels and heavier and more frequent rain. As global temperatures rise, many places, including major cities such as New York, Shanghai and Bangkok, will be threatened by flooding.

◄ In many parts of the world, the glaciers that people depend on for water are melting fast. These glaciers in Peru, South America, are threatened by both climate change and mining activities. The area covered by glaciers has shrunk by 25 per cent in the last 30 years.

Losing lakes and rivers

As the demand for water rises and we divert more water from the water cycle for industry and domestic use, many of our lakes and rivers are in danger of drying up. As well as losing the water supply, many fish and other freshwater species have been lost or are endangered.

North America's Great Lakes

The Great Lakes of North America contain 20 per cent of the world's fresh surface water. As a result of a combination of a changing climate and an increasing demand for the lakes' water, levels are becoming dangerously low. In the summer of 2007 Lake Superior dropped to its lowest level in 80 years. The water loss has damaged wetlands, hit production at power plants and hampered shipping and other boating activities.

Low water levels also affect the lakes' wildlife. Coaster brook trout used to swim in their millions in the Great Lakes but their numbers have now decreased to such an extent that they may soon be listed as an endangered species.

HOTSPOT:

The Yellow River

Millions of people in northern China face water shortages as the level of the Yellow River falls. Booming industries, drought and general overuse have left the Yellow River (right) so drained that in recent summer low seasons it has dried up before reaching the sea.

Lake Mead

Lake Mead is one of the largest water reservoirs in the world. It was created by the construction of the Hoover Dam on the Colorado River, in the USA, and when full contains about 36 trillion litres of water. The water in the lake irrigates about 6,000 square km of farmland and provides HEP for about 500,000 homes. If current trends continue, the lake may dry up completely by 2057, meaning the cities of Las Vegas, Los Angeles and San Diego will be very short of water.

Water loss to industry

Mongolia is a land-locked country in east Asia that is hundreds of kilometres from the sea. In the last five years over 1,200 of its rivers and 2,600 of its lakes have dried up. Much of this is thought to have been caused by its water-intensive leather tanning and gold mining industries.

⊽ The water level in Lake Mead has been dropping for 10 years due to a continued drought in the south-western USA and the increasing demand from the local growing population. In this picture you can clearly see where the maximum level of the lake once was.

Pollution

Another cause of water shortage is **pollution**. Human activities have polluted and reduced freshwater supplies in many parts of the world.

Water can be polluted in many ways. **Pesticides** and **fertilisers** used in farming can often end up in rivers, as can dangerous industrial pollutants. In many developing countries untreated sewage is often the biggest form of water pollution.

Pollution from farming

Fertilisers are used to improve soil quality and make crops grow better. When too much fertiliser is applied it can run off the land into rivers. This makes the water extra-rich in **nutrients** and plants and algae grow quickly. They use up all the oxygen and block out the light. This kills fish and other aquatic life.

⊙ Asian rivers are the most polluted in the world. In this picture, industrial waste water leaks into the Bei Xizohe River in Beijing, China.

Pesticides are also used in agriculture. They can be highly toxic and are dangerous to wildlife and humans if they reach the waterways. Although the use of these chemicals is closely monitored, the pressure on farmers to produce more and more food means that agriculture is still the biggest source of water pollutants.

Pollution from sewage

Dirty water should be sent to a sewage works and cleaned before it can be released back into the environment. However many developing countries do not have water-treatment facilities. In some countries, up to 90 per cent of raw sewage is thought to enter the water system without any treatment at all. This not only pollutes the water and makes it undrinkable, but it also creates conditions in which diseases such as cholera and typhoid can spread (also see page 13).

(also see page 13)

⊙ The canal network in Bangkok, Thailand, is both a transportation system and an open sewer.

Wars over water

As water supplies become scarcer, water will become a resource that is fought over more often. It is possible that water disputes could even lead to war in some parts of the world.

Local disputes

In Kenya there have been arguments between herders and farmers as increasing quantities of water are taken from traditional watering holes and used for agriculture. In 2005 a dispute between Kikuyu farmers and Maasai cattle herders resulted in two weeks of violence and the deaths of more than 20 people.

⊙ Nomadic cattle herders in Africa have relied on traditional watering holes for centuries. Having to share what they consider to be their water with agricultural farmers has led to some violent disputes.

Damage by dams

Water disputes can be caused by the building of dams. When the Aswan Dam was built across the River Nile in Egypt in 1971 it seemed to be a great asset to the area. The people of Egypt had plenty of clean water, an HEP station provided electricity for homes and factories all over the country and farmers had water supplies to irrigate their crops. But there were also disadvantages. The dam stopped the yearly flood of nutrient-rich sediment that used to provide farmers in the river valley below with healthy, fertile soils. Now farmers have to rely on chemical fertilisers which raises the cost of the crops they grow. The increase in use of fertilisers has also led to higher levels of pollution downstream.

International problems

About 160 million people in ten countries depend on the River Nile, and rights to its water are constantly being argued over. Egypt and Sudan are the largest consumers of the Nile's water, but the other eight countries want their share of the water allowance increased. A new water-sharing arrangement was discussed in July 2009 but no agreement was reached. The population in the Nile basin is expected to double in the next 25 years, so claims for a share of the Nile's water can only increase.

⊚ The River Nile is one of the longest rivers in the world. It provides drinking water for millions of people and irrigates hundreds of thousands of square kilometres of agricultural land. It is one of the world's most valuable water resources and is constantly being fought over.

Finding new supplies

Our planet is not short of water – it is just short of the right sort of water. Too much of it is in a form that we cannot use; in the atmosphere, in ice and in the sea. We need to find ways of using this water.

Cloud seeding

Cloud seeding is a method of forcing clouds to produce rain. It is done by dispersing substances into the air that cause the water vapour to condense into rain drops. The most common chemicals used for cloud seeding are silver iodide or frozen carbon dioxide. This method is quite successful at producing rain in dry areas, but it is expensive and there can be environmental side-effects. In Australia the process was banned after it was found that populations of the pygmy possum were being affected by silver poisoning.

⊙ Cloud seeding can be done by ground generators or by plane. Although its main purpose is to increase rainfall, it is also used in ski resorts to produce snow, and at airports to clear fog.

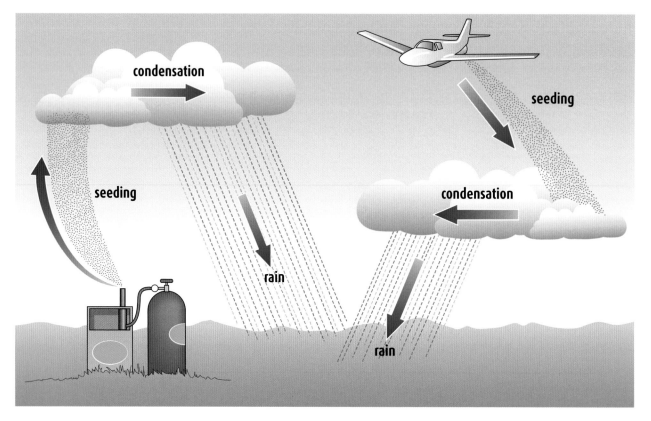

Drinking icebergs?

Scientists have looked into the idea of towing icebergs from polar regions to countries that are suffering water shortages. Iceberg water would be clean, non-salty and free of pollution. A trial was carried out in southern Chile in the 1990s, but it was not successful due to expensive costs and an 80 per cent loss of the volume of ice. However, some wealthy, desert countries such as Saudi Arabia are still interested in the idea.

Desalination

Desalination is the process of removing salt from seawater to make fresh water. The process could provide the world with all the water it needs, since the supply of seawater is limitless. However it is an expensive process and does have some polluting by-products such as very salty waste water which has to be disposed of. In some desalination plants table salt can be produced as a by-product. Desalination is carried out in several countries including the USA, Australia, India and Saudi Arabia. The world's largest desalination plant is in the United Arab Emirates.

HOTSPOT:
Desalination in Spain

A desalination plant has opened near Barcelona, Spain (below). It will provide 200 million litres of drinking water daily for the city's 4.5 million people. It produces 45 litres of drinking water from each 100 litres of seawater.

Water conservation

The population of the world is increasing and is expected to rise from nearly seven billion to nine billion in just a few decades. Some predictions say that more than half of the people in the world will be suffering water scarcity by 2030 unless water use can be managed in a more **sustainable** way.

Most of the world's developed countries are lucky to be in areas of high rainfall and plentiful water. Any water shortages that they suffer are likely to be caused by bad water management. There are many ways in which they could save water.

Improving water efficiency

Water companies are responsible for supplying water, for keeping the quality of water at a high level and for maintaining the network of pipes and storage facilities around the country. Many water networks are old and leaky and need to be repaired. In some countries over 30 per cent of water is lost as a result of leakages in the water system.

⊙ A superstore in the UK has a rainwater recycling system. This monitor allows customers to see exactly how many litres of rainwater are used each day.

HOTSPOT:
Stormwater harvesting

The Coca-Cola company in Sydney, Australia has developed a scheme which will catch the rain falling on the roofs of their warehouses. The water collected will be used for flushing toilets, irrigating a council park and some will be treated to be used as drinking water. The project will save nine million litres of water a year.

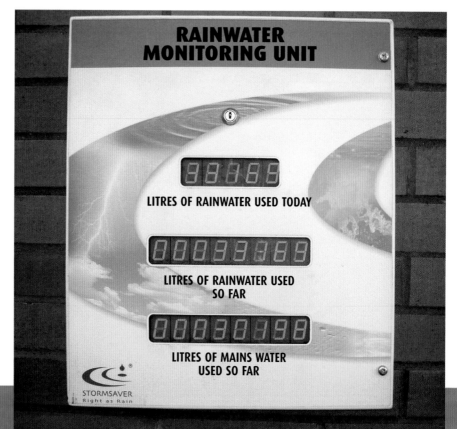

RAINWATER MONITORING UNIT

LITRES OF RAINWATER USED TODAY

LITRES OF RAINWATER USED SO FAR

LITRES OF MAINS WATER USED SO FAR

STORMSAVER
Right as Rain

Saving water at home

Many households in the UK pay a set fee for their water. This means they can use as much as they like without paying more. This system does not encourage water conservation. In places where houses have water meters and customers pay for the amount of water they actually use, people are much less wasteful. They think about the amount of water they are using and whether it is really necessary.

Saving water in industry

Most farms and industries do pay for their water using meters, so it makes sense for them to try to reduce the amount they use. Many industries have reduced the amount of water they use by reusing and recycling water, and by redesigning their production processes to need less water.

Our water resources may be under pressure, but if we look after them more carefully and use them in a more sustainable way, our supplies will be able to support the world's growing population.

The Bear River Solar Aquatics Wastewater Treatment Facility, in Nova Scotia, Canada, is the first solar aquatic treatment facility in North America. It turns waste water into fresh water by passing it through a series of tanks containing bacteria, algae, snails, fish and plants. Over 60 million litres of water are treated this way each year.

Glossary

Arid
A very dry climate or place.

Atmosphere
The layer of gases that surrounds the Earth.

Cholera
A disease caused by drinking contaminated drinking water.

Condense
Change from a gas into a liquid.

Developed countries
Countries that have a high standard of living and an industrial economy.

Developing countries
Poorer countries where people have a low standard of living and low levels of industry.

Efficiency
A measurement of how well something works.

Evaporation
The change from a liquid into a gas.

Fertilisers
Chemicals that are put on fields to encourage crops to grow better.

Genetically modified
When a plant has had its genes modified or changed by human action.

Global warming
A rise in the average temperature of the Earth which some people think is caused by an increase of greenhouse gases in the atmosphere.

Groundwater
The water present in the Earth's rocks and underground streams.

Hydroelectric
Electricity generated by the power of water.

Industrial Revolution
A period in the late 18th and early 19th centuries when Western Europe changed from being an agricultural to an industrial nation.

Infrastructure
The basic structure or features of a system or organisation.

Irrigate
To supply water to crops to encourage their growth.

Nutrients
Substances that help plants and animals grow better.

Pesticides
Chemicals that are sprayed onto crops to kill pests.

Pollution
Anything that makes the environment dirty.

Rainforest
A forest in a tropical area where there is warmth and a lot of rain.

Resource
A naturally-occuring material that is useful to us.

Run-off
Water from rain or irrigation that runs over the surface of the ground rather than soaking in.

Sanitation
The provision of clean water and drainage facilities in order to protect health.

Sewage
Liquid and solid waste from buildings that should be carried away in drains.

Sustainable
Something that is capable of being continued without running out or damaging the environment.

Textile
Cloth or fabrics made by weaving or knitting.

Typhoid
An illness caused by drinking dirty water which spreads quickly and can affect a lot of people.

Water scarcity
A lack of water in an area caused by drought or overuse.

Water stress
When more water is needed than that available.

Water vapour
Water droplets suspended in the air.

Yields
The amount produced.

Further information

Books

Water Cycle (Earth Cycles)
Franklin Watts, 2009

Water Supply (How It Works)
James Nixon, Franklin Watts, 2009

Water Supplies in Crisis (Planet in Crisis)
Steve Parker and Russ Parker, Rosen Central, 2009

Threats to Our Water Supply (Can the Earth Survive?)
Louise A Spilsbury, Rosen Publishing Group, 2009

Using Water (Green Team)
Sally Hewitt, Franklin Watts, 2008

Websites

www.watereducation.org/doc.asp?id=1022#HowMuchWater

How much water does it take to brush your teeth? Wash the car? Run the washing machine? Learn the answers to these questions and ways that you can help reduce water wastage at this website.

ga.water.usgs.gov/edu/earthwherewater.html

A website about Water Science for Schools. Discover how much water there is on Earth. Investigate the water cycle and where all the water we use goes.

www.wateraid.org/uk/what_we_do/how_we_work/default.asp

Water Aid UK works around the world creating sustainable water and sanitation services. Keep up to date with their work by signing up to their e-newsletter.

Index